BROWSING

BROWSING

By John Barth
Linoleum cuts by Mary Rhinelander

"Inasmuch and insofar as the world is regardable
as a pointless web of virtually infinite interconnections,
anything in it (including this book) may serve
as the browser's point of entry."

The Literary House Press
Washington College
Chestertown, Maryland
2004

In Chestertown, Maryland, not far from where I write these lines, is a good small liberal-arts college to which the Father of Our Country kindly lent his name upon its establishment in 1782. My wife and I often use its library when we're in residence at Langford Creek; for that reason, although I like to keep a low profile hereabouts, in the fall of 1992 I was pleased to contribute to the below-described public celebration the following address.

My congratulations to Washington College and to the staff of its Clifton Miller Library on the acquisition of this library's 200,000th volume. My thanks to whoever took it into their heads to invite me to help celebrate that occasion, and equally to you all for troubling yourselves to come hear what I have to say.

I confess to have been a little curious on that score

myself; that's why I accepted the library's invitation. I am in rigorous accord with E. M. Forster's rhetorical question "How can I tell what I think until I see what I say?" Indeed, I learned recently[1] that that eloquent *obiter dictum* of Forster's has been updated and elaborated by contemporary neuroscience and language theory into what's known as the Pandemonium model of Utterance – a model that theorizes multiple goals or intentions percolating through our consciousness, on the lookout, so to speak, for materials of expression, while at the same time those materials of expression (what zoologist Richard Dawkins calls "memes," or memory units), likewise distributed through our brains, are reciprocally vigilant for opportunities of incorporation. What issues from this ongoing, low-level pandemonium inside our heads is what in fact we end up saying or writing – which then we may have to qualify immediately because we see that it's not quite what we meant; perhaps (as T. S. Eliot says) that "that is not it, at all." Contrariwise, we may recognize it to be *exactly* what we think and believe, now that we see how it has gotten itself said.

I don't know how it is with you, but the Pandemonium Model of Utterance certainly reminds me of how things happen in *my* head, and likewise at my writing table. Not to wander irretrievably far from the subject of our celebration, let's imagine individual consciousness as a sort of open library stack (what we call our memory) whose "books" are itching to be borrowed. Our intentions are half-random, half-purposive browsers through that open stack, and our utterances are the more or less serendipitous matchup of books and borrowers: a matchup continuously "feedback-guided, error-corrected, and gain-adjusted" (in the words of Daniel C. Dennett), but never without an essential, inescapable element of browser-like serendipity, whatever the urgency and the momentousness of the occasion. It is a matchup, moreover, in which not only are the "borrowers" more or less modified by the "books" (as is often the case with literal book borrowers), but conversely, as any librarian can attest to be sometimes the literal case too – the book somewhat modified by its borrower.

The book that I myself most recently borrowed from the Miller Library, for example, is a study of the great sixteenth-century French comic writer François Rabelais by the great contemporary Russian critic Mikhail Bakhtin. It is an utterly humorless (though quite brilliant) examination of the millennia-old tradition of folk humor – the rough, democratic, "Rabelaisian" humor of marketplace and carnival – to which Rabelais gave magnificent literary expression in

Gargantua and Pantagruel. Mikhail Bakhtin's book has substantially altered the way I think about François Rabelais – and evidently it impressed some earlier borrower of the volume as well, for he or she altered it by ticking certain passages in the margins and even bracketing a few of them in the text, with the consequence that I found myself interacting not only with Bakhtin's interaction with Rabelais, but also with some prior borrower's interaction with Bakhtin's interaction. Now, I happen to believe that anyone who marks up a library book deserves Islamic justice; all the same, it was a spooky and not uninteresting experience to notice early on that my fore-reader was ticking pretty consistently the very passages I would have ticked, were I a ticker of passages in library books. Soon enough it became a kind of game between me and him/her: How come you didn't tick *this* passage, which I think is memorable indeed? How come you bracketed this other one, which doesn't strike me as all that dazzling an aperçu? Maybe I'd better run it through my head again. . . .

In short, the reader had changed the book, as well as vice versa, and I was reading that reader as well as reading the writer and, by extension, reading the writer that that writer was writing about. This complex transaction took place on the beach at Ocean City

in the last week of August, by the way, and despite my best efforts to keep the Atlantic away from Mikhail Bakhtin and François Rabelais and my anonymous co-reader of *Rabelais and His World*,[2] a bit of salt water dripped onto the lower front cover. As that happens to be exactly where my left ring finger rests when I read,

I too have very slightly changed the book that very slightly changed me: There's a worn spot there that wasn't there when I borrowed the book – but I doubt that that alteration will significantly alter some future borrower of Bakhtin-on-Rabelais.

The Pandemonium Model of Utterance, I was saying: that dating service for Intentions and Materials of Expression. I hope to wander back to the browserish aspect of human consciousness, human verbalization – I would go so far as to say human identity, even – after I've browsed through some other alcoves of my subject, which, right about here in the early drafting of these remarks, I realized was going to be *browsing*, and so decided to make browsing my method as well as my subject matter: This is what aestheticians call "significant form" and I call the Principle of Metaphoric Means. To browse means "to inspect in a leisurely and casual way" (so runs the verb's first definition in my dictionary, which etymologizes it back to the Old French *broust*, meaning a twig or shoot). Also and therefore, it means "to feed on leaves and young shoots" (the second definition) – your mode of sustenance if you happen to be a deer, a goat, or a giraffe, for example, or an undecided but decidedly curious undergraduate. Of this, too, more presently: young sprouts browsing through the leaves of books. Libraries have this happy arboreal aspect: Not only do they themselves have branches and even twigs – e.g., the Rock Hall Branch and the Galena Twig of our Kent County Library – but the word "book" itself is an etymological offshoot of "beech," which is how their pages come to be called "leaves" and those who forage therethrough "browsers."

Well. Browsing thus through the *Bs* in my desk dictionary to check out the word *browse* reminded me that it was while browsing through the *Bs* in the card catalogue and literature stacks of the Pattee Library of the Pennsylvania State University, where I happened to be teaching at the time, that I serendipitously encountered the writings of the great contemporary Argentine Jorge Luis Borges, whose fiction I had begun to hear interesting things about but hadn't read yet. A writer's muse from time to time whispers, "You'd better check this one out"; I always follow her advice, but not always promptly. I was there among the *Bs*, I confess, partly to see whether my own books were included in the library's holdings; there were just three of them back then, and the experience of being a card-catalogued novelist was still rather heady. I don't remember whether I found myself there that day or not (what one hopes to find is one's books in the catalogue but not on the shelf); I do remember discovering Borges, a writer who came strongly to affect the way I thought about contemporary fiction, my own included, and numerous other things as well. In one of his marvelous stories, for example,[3] Borges defines "money" as "a collection of possible futures." That's how I feel about libraries: A library is a collection of possible futures. My own future was significantly course-corrected, not for the first or last time, by that fortuitous encounter in the Penn State stacks.

Señor Borges, I believe, shared my feeling about libraries (for a time he was a librarian himself, at the National Library in Buenos Aries). Another of his *ficciones*, called "The Library of Babel," involves an infinite library, whose innumerable volumes contain every possible combination of alphabetical characters and spaces. Such a library – the verbal equivalent of Lucretius's universe, comprising an infinite quantity of a finite variety of atoms in every possible combination

– would therefore include the record not only of "actual" history, but likewise of all imaginable histories; it would contain not only the true prediction of the future, but, alas, the prediction of every possible and impossible future. I say "alas" because in the infinite Library of Babel we would have no way of distinguishing, before the fact, the accurate prediction from all the slightly or grossly inaccurate ones. The truth would be there, somewhere, but only extraordinary chance or special dispensation would lead us to it.

Metaphorically speaking, of course, that is the case with all libraries, despite the best efforts of the most knowledgeable and sophisticated staff and the highest-tech database search programs, for the reason that every general library represents and indeed more or less contains the accumulated mental resources of civilization. In the granary of the past are the seeds of the future, and no doubt the best way to assure a crop is to make the widest possible assortment of cultivars as accessible as possible to as many as possible within the community that the library serves.

The image of Borges's infinite library (along with the phrase "widest possible assortment of cultivars," which I chose because it's not every day that a novelist

gets to use the word "cultivars") moves me to browse a bit around the number that occasions our present occasion: *200,000* books. Is that a lot of books? Quite a few books? "Right many," as we Eastern Shore folk sometimes say? Only a few? Too many? Just enough? Unanswerable questions, on the face of them, but some other book numbers might help us put ours in perspective. A browse through the *World Almanac* tells us that if we add another nine million volumes to our 200,000, we'll match the stacks of the New York Public Library – the research stacks only. Add another seventy million to that (we're talking 79,200,000 *items* this time, not necessarily volumes), and we approximate the holdings of the Library of Congress. Throughout most of recorded history, on the other hand, 200,000 would have constituted a world-class library: A browse through the wonderful old eleventh edition of the *Encyclopaedia Britannica* reminds or teaches us that the great library of Pergamum, for example, in Asia Minor, second only in its day to the fabled library of Alexandria, at the peak of its flourishing boasted some 200,000 "volumes" – scrolls, they would have been, of papyrus and of vellum parchment; scrolls to be *rolled* and un*rolled*, from the Latin verb for which action we get our word "volume" and the Swedes get their word *Volvo*. ("Parchment," by the way, comes from

Pergamum both historically and etymologically. I don't mind smarting off to you about these things, because many of them I just learned myself, browsing around for this talk.) Plutarch tells us that when Mark Antony's Roman legions captured the city of Pergamum in Fortysomething B.C., Antony made a gift of those 200,000 scrolls to his friend Cleopatra to add to the holdings of that already-legendary library of hers in Alexandria, part of which had been burned by Caesar's fleet a couple of years earlier.

Well, books *are* nice love-gifts. Two hundred thousand of them might strike some of us as a touch much, a touch over-magnificent, but Aristotle lists "magnificence" among the moral virtues in his *Nichomachean Ethics*; the classical Romans went in for the grand gesture, and in this instance it seems to have had the intended effect. Anyhow, think of trying to select *one book* as a knock-your-socks-off love gift to the owner of the largest library in the world. I like to imagine a whole fleet of triremes ferrying those 200,000 scrolls from Pergamum to Alexandria along with a nicely understated cover note: *Thinking of you. Mark. XXXI October, XL-something B.C.*

More numbers: the fiction department of the Barths' personal library on a branch of Langford Creek (we call it our Branch library) has evolved into a steady-state operation of about 1,300 volumes, plus or minus several dozen. Its size is constrained by the fixed amount of shelf space that my wife and I allot to that particular category of literature. Every couple of years we do a triage on the overflow, mostly new novels sent by their publisher in hope of a blurb: *This* one we'll keep, because we hope to get around to reading it someday; *that* one we really must keep whether we read it or not, since the author has inscribed it to us. On the other hand, no way we're likely ever to get to *this* one and *that* one, even though they might turn out to be wonderful or important or both: the books of the decade (if they do, we'll borrow them from some other library in some future decade). For every "new" book we keep, we cull an "old" one from the shelves – old and new in terms of acquisition, not date of composition. The number remains approximately constant; the quality curve, we like to think, gently rises. As for the worthy dispossessed, we donate them to our favorite *Salon des refusés*, the library of the O'Neill Literary House,[4] for some apprentice writer on the browse to serendip into.

Because who can say what half-random combination of voices from here, there, and anywhere might happen to inspire a new singer? I know of one instance where a thirteenth-century Persian fabulator

(Scheherazade) interbred with, among others, a nineteenth-century Brazilian romantic formalist (Joaquim Machado de Assis) and an early-twentieth-century Irish Modernist (James Joyce) to produce a contemporary American Postmodernist. Most of that wild cross-pollination took place in the classics stacks of the old Gilman Hall Library at Johns Hopkins, where I used to work as a book filer to help defray my undergraduate tuition, and where I managed to read quite a lot of what I was supposed to be returning from cart to shelf: my à la carte education. Library stacks, in their quiet way, can be really swinging places; virtual orgies of cross-cultural insemination go on there, at all hours. If Jesse Helms and Pat Robertson get wind of it, the American Library Association is in for trouble.

Speaking of which (apprentice writers and book numbers, I mean, not virtual orgies), Gustave Flaubert famously remarked that it is enough for a writer to have read five or six books well. He neglected to tell us which five or six, however, and so I caution apprentice writers that only the massively well read, like Flaubert, are entitled to make such dismissive remarks, just as only Nobel Prize-winners are allowed to sniff at the Nobel Prize. (I've heard it said, by the way, that a certain distinguished theoretical physicist, toward the close of his career, once lamented to an interviewer that by his own standards he had never had a really good idea in his professional lifetime. The surprised interviewer asked, "Do you mean a Nobel Prize-winning idea?" "No no no," said the physicist: "I mean a *really* great idea." The disparagement would be more pungent coming from a Nobel laureate – except that the anecdote happens to not be tellable that way.)

How many books are enough? When one of my graduate students asked Donald Barthelme, who was visiting our seminar, what she might do to become a better writer, Barthelme suggested that she might begin by reading all of philosophy, from the pre-Socratics up to last semester. The young woman objected that I had already urged her comrades to read all of literature, from the Egyptian Middle Kingdom up to last semester, in order to get some sense of the turf. "That, too," Barthelme said. "You're probably wasting time on things like eating and sleeping. Cease that, and go read everything." Thomas Wolfe, if I remember correctly, attempted to do just that in his New York years, and was rendered desperate by the fact that the Serious Lit stacks alone of the New York Public grew at a rate enormously faster than even a speed reader could hope to approach.

To wind up this exercise in number-browsing: At

the opposite pole we have a reading list even shorter than Flaubert's unspecified *"cinq ou six livres"*: that of those Islamic fundamentalists who maintain that only *one* book is necessary, the holy Koran, inasmuch as all the others either agree with it, in which case they're redundancies, or else disagree with it, in which case they're heresies. Christian fundamentalism has sometimes inclined that way too, substituting "the Book" for the Koran – although "Bible", strictly speaking, comes from the Greek plural *biblia*, meaning books: the books of the Book, to be sure, not just any old plurality of books.[5] The Arabic *alcoran*, on the other hand, means not the book but "the reading," or recitation, while the Hebrew *Torah* means "the law," or instruction. I don't doubt that subtle and exemplary differences among Christian, Islamic, and Judaic cultures might be extrapolated from these different meanings of their terms for their scriptures, but I'm certainly not going to attempt any such extrapolation – and I'll spare you an aria on the interesting word "extrapolate."[6]

So: Given these numerical extremes – the single-volume library of fundamentalist Islam on the one hand, Borges's infinite Library of Babel on the other – how big should a library be? Specifically, the general library of a good small liberal arts college like this one?

The only acceptable answer is "as big as possible," for while the quality of the collection is no doubt more important than its size, there's much to be said for mere muchness, for raw magnitude. George Boas, the late aesthetician and historian of ideas at Johns Hopkins (and my mentor, although he didn't know it), used to fret about "great books" curricula because they tend to leave out the books that disagree with the Great Books. The reading of non-great books, Boas believed, even of downright bad books – even of inexcusably, unredeemedly wicked books – is important to a truly liberal education: liberal as in "liberating," as in *Veritas vos liberabit*, "The truth shall make you free," which happens to be the motto both of my alma mater and of the United States Central Intelligence Agency, neither of which means it in quite the same spirit that Jesus intended in the gospel of St. John, Chapter 8, Verse 32. The *liber* of "liberal" and "liberate," I remark in passing, is an entirely different root from the *liber* of "library," but the two roots indisputably nourish the same tree.

Let's hear it, then, for raw magnitude: I can testify that my undergraduate book-filing days in the orderly labyrinth of Greek and Roman classics and of William Foxwell Albright's Oriental Seminary (which back then comprised Sanskrit, Persian, Arabic, Hebrew, Egyptian, and various other literatures) indelibly impressed me with the sheer size and diversity of the *already said*, and made me a cultural pluralist for life – without, mirabile dictu, intimidating me into respectful silence. If you happen to be a refugee from the Dorchester County tide marshes (another sort of labyrinth), as I was and remain, and particularly if you aspire to keep one foot at least ankle deep back in your native bog while the other foot traipses through the wider world, it is well to have such an off-the-cart smorgasbord under your belt, for ballast.

As big as possible, then, your library, the absolute minimum requirement being that it be big enough for a habitual browser to get lost in.

How big is that? We seem to be back where we started: How many books does it take to lose your average seasoned, half-purposive browser? Sometimes, as has been demonstrated, just one will do the trick. I find a good dictionary or almanac or encyclopedia as difficult to extricate myself from as a good hardware or marine supply store; from any of them I'm likely to emerge with something very different from what I went in for. I even resist interrupting a sentence in progress to check out one of its items in such seductive reference works, lest I mislay the thread that led me into the labyrinth and find myself lost in the funhouse of the *Britannica* or the *Oxford English Dictionary*.

Is this another sort of one-book fundamentalism? Not at all, for the reasons that in this case the "scripture" involved is humanly compiled, not divinely revealed; that it deals in worldish information, not heavenly truths; that it's not a labyrinth, really, but a network, leading always as much back out into the world as on to its own farther interconnections. Such secular scriptures, it's worth noting, needn't be reference works. When James Joyce was asked, late in his career, whether he didn't after all demand too much of his readers, the author of *Ulysses* and *Finnegans Wake* is said to have replied, "I demand nothing of my readers, except that they devote the rest of their lives to my books." – and indeed, one could profitably do just that with such a work as *Finnegans Wake*, precisely because in addition to leading always further into itself it leads always out of itself: to the rest of literature, to myth, history, languages, the sciences, virtually the whole spectrum of human knowledge and experience. To "master" such an "encyclopedic" text would require a degree of knowledge and understanding approaching the global – but then, if I remember correctly, that is just about what Lord Tennyson says about the prerequisites for understanding a simple flower in a crannied wall: "I

hold you here, root and all, in my hand, / Little flower
– but *if* I could understand / What you are, root and
all, and all in all, / I should know what God and man
is." Inasmuch and insofar as the world is regardable as
a seamless web of virtually infinite interconnections,
anything in it (including any book) may serve as the
browser's point of entry – so long as, unlike some
scriptural fundamentalists, we keep the connections
open to the rest of the web, the rest of the labyrinth,
funhouse, library, network, world.

A better answer to the question "How big need a
library be for one to get happily and perhaps even
profitably lost in it?" would be "Big enough to consti-
tute a network of interconnections sufficiently rich to
serve as a model of the mentally apprehensible world."
That formulation – in particular the term *network* –
leads or at least invites me to the all-but-final twigs of
this little browse through the subject of browsing.

I've been speaking of *books*, mainly, as one still
tends to do when speaking of libraries. Our occasion,
after all, is this library's acquisition of its 200,000th
book;[7] there was probably a similar hurrah at
Pergamum in Fortysomething B.C. when the 200,000th
scroll joined their collection, just before Mark Antony

closed in as Cleopatra's field agent for acquisitions. But every frequenter of libraries knows that the image of the library as a book museum, or even as a storehouse of the printed word, is a severely limited image indeed, not only because audiovisual materials are so important a part of any modern library's resources – cassettes, slides, microfilms, laser disks, and the like – but also because more and more of the library's available supply of "written" language is "accessed" these days not directly off the shelf and the page but via modems and video display terminals. For a great many research purposes, the printed book – that handy-dandy object that we cuddle up with on the beach or airplane or recliner chair and try not to deface with suntan lotions and marginalia unless it's our personal copy – is often less useful than the computerized database, the search program, and the electronic network: technologies that are obliging to us to rethink our familiar book-oriented notions of "text," "author," "reader," "copyright," and the like. In the scientific community, especially, but in the humanities and other areas as well, research findings are exchanged, "papers" are "written" and peer-reviewed and revised and enlarged or subsumed, without there necessarily being any officially "published," canonical text at all. There are electronic journals (by which term we do not mean magazines about electronics); there are even on-line literary periodicals, not to mention all sorts of interlinkages among specialized databases. Ever more frequently, our transactions with the "already said" – and with colleagues, business associates, even geographically distant family members or fellow enthusiasts of some particular pursuit – take place not in library stacks of printed books or in any other literal space with literal texts, but in the virtual or hyperspaces of computer networks, with virtual rather than literal hard-copy "finished" texts. Even, we are beginning to see, with hypertexts.

What is hyperspace? What are hypertexts? For any of you still unfamiliar with these phenomena, it is fortunately too late in this talk – too late in life, I suspect, for some of us print-loving troglodytes perfectly comfortable with the mature but threatened technologies and institutions of books, publishers, authors, readers, and copyright laws – too late for me to do more than browse the very edges of the subject.

Most of us have experienced to some extent the "virtual reality" or "virtual worlds" of computer modelings and simulations, which seem to be used these days in virtually every field of human enterprise from weather forecasting to market research. And whether we employ the term or not, most of us are familiar with the "virtual texts" – unprinted, unfinalized, ever open to emendations small or large— that float about in our word processors or in the hyperspace between our computers and those of our editors, colleagues, accomplices, fellow accessees to some electronic network or other. Now imagine a "text" (the word is already in quotes, the signal or symptom of virtuality) every word of which – at least many a key word of which – is a window or point of entry into a network of associated "texts" (or graphics, music, statistics, spoken language, whatever a computer can reproduce), these several networks themselves interconnected and infinitely modifiable – or *virtually* infinitely so – by "readers" who can enter the text at any point, trace any of a zillion paths through its associated micro- and macro-networks, add or subtract material and modify the linkages as they please, and then exit at any point, in the process having been virtual co-authors or co-editors as well as "readers" of their virtual text. That's hypertext.

The quick brown fox jumps over the lazy dog. Imagine a "loaded" display of that innocent proposition on your computer monitor, such that "clicking" on any item in it opens a window menu of associations available for exploring, from the relative nimbleness of temperate-zone quadrupeds, through the history of fox hunting and its representation in painting, music, and literature, to soundtracks of hounds in full cry (with or without expert commentary) and disquisitions on animal rights – and every one of those associated "lexias," as the hypertexties call them, similarly loaded, another ring of keys with which one may open yet further doors, and on and on and on – no two routes through the maze ever likely to be the same, and every venturer thereinto not only a Theseus but a Daedalus, remodeling the labyrinth at will en route through it. That's hypertext, more or less, and it alarms and intrigues me at least as much as I hope it alarms and intrigues you, and we're likely to be hearing a lot more about it before this weary century expires, because whether or not it's more hype than text (as some naysayers allege), its impassioned prophets proclaim it to be the third great revolution in language technology, after the invention of writing and the invention of moveable type.[8] So watch out.

Hypertext is, I suppose, the ultimate form of browsing. In our virtual way, we library-browsers have been virtually hypertexting all along without realizing it, the way Molière's Monsieur Jourdain comes to realize that he's been speaking prose all his life without knowing it. My mental interaction on the beach at Ocean City with that previous borrower's shamelessly marginated interaction with Mikhail Bakhtin's extended interactions with all previous commentators' critical interactions with the text of François Rabelais's literary interaction with the world of sixteenth-century France can be thought of as a somewhat awkward and limited linear analogue to hypertext browsing, which is essentially non-linear. And for the past forty-odd minutes, you all have been the patient attendants upon such another limited linear analogue: namely, this demonstrational browse through the subject of browsing, which could as easily have followed any number of other serial associations than the ones that it turns out to have followed – except that I happened to have the destination *hypertext* in mind, and so my interlinkages had the aspect more of waypoints than of innocent, freestanding young shoots to be randomly browsed.

But true browsing, QED, is always only partly random. Those "innocent young shoots" that the browser browses upon aren't really freestanding; they're multiply interconnected by a complex network of underground rhizomes, like spartina canes in a marsh or wire grass in your garden or the axons and dendrites of the multibillion neurons of our brains: a network unapparent and scarcely apprehensible until we begin to browse along one of its all-but-infinite possible pathways, sighing, perhaps, at the number of alternative routes that we don't have time to explore. I spoke earlier of the "arboreal" aspect of libraries – their branches and twigs, the etymology of words like *book* – and now I've mentioned rhizomes. It happens that the terms "arborescent" and "rhizomatic" are fashionable just now in post-structuralist literary theory, employed[9] to describe two very different kinds of organizing structures. Libraries are "arborescent" not only in their aforenoted woodsy associations, but in their hierarchical classification of verbal subject matter into mainstem categories with multiply branching subcategories and sub-subcategories (the Dewey decimal system of book classification is an elaborate instance of arborescent structure). But browsing, like hypertext, is essentially "rhizomatic," as is the human brain and the world apprehended by it. Whatever its official place in some hierarchical system, every mental datum and sensory image, like every word in a language, is also a node in a rhizomatic network that may lead to illuminating, beautiful, useful, or at least unexpected interconnections.

Now that I've seen what I've said on the subject of browsing, I believe I know what I think: that I want to end this talk back in a library with the great Jorge Luis Borges, whose texts may not be hyper, but are often very super. One of my favorites among them is set in what used to be called Czechoslovakia in 1938 and involves a not especially successful writer named Jaromir Hladík, who is condemned to death by the Nazis for the crime of being Jewish. On his last night on earth, Hladik prays for time to complete an unfinished work in progress, and toward dawn he has a crucial dream:

> ...he dreamt he had hidden himself in one of the naves of the Clementine Library. A librarian wearing dark glasses asked him: What are you looking for? Hladík answered: *God.* The Librarian told him:
> *God is in one of the letters on one of the pages of one of the 400,000 volumes of the Clementine. My fathers and fathers of my fathers have sought after that letter. I've gone blind looking for it.* He removed his glasses,[10] and Hladík saw that his eyes were dead. A reader came in to return an atlas. *This atlas is useless,* he said, and handed it to Hladík, who opened it at random. As if through a haze, he saw a map of India. With a sudden rush of assurance, he touched one of the tiniest letters. An ubiquitous voice said: *The time for your work has been granted.*

The story in which this dream occurs is called, in English, "The Secret Miracle"; it has a magnificent ending, which I won't give away. I exhort those of you who don't know it to look it up, here in your splendid 200,000-volume library (already half the size of the fabled Clementine). Do not let the circulation staff look it up or fetch it for you; go into the stacks yourself, with only the most general directions, and do not rush to the correct address. Stroll the neighborhood; handle the merchandise; see what catches your eye. You are not likely to find God while browsing through the stacks of the Clifton M. Miller Library – though who knows? What you might just possibly find, however, is yourself.

NOTES

1. From Daniel C. Dennett's *Consciousness Explained* (Boston: Little, Brown, 1991).

2. Cambridge, MA: M.I.T. Press, 1968.

3. "The Zahir."

4. Washington College's enviable sanctuary for apprentice writers, most of them in pursuit of the staggering Sophie Kerr Prize.

5. In pre-Gutenburg terms we speak of Book Such-and-Such of the *Iliad* or the *Aeneid*: their several scrolled "chapters." The Pergamum library's 200,000 "volumes," therefore, would not have equaled the 200,000 post-Gutenburg books of the Clifton M. Miller Library.

6. Literally to "polish out of."

7. The volume officially so designated in this instance was a signed copy of H.L. Mencken's *Treatise on the Gods,* presented to the Miller Library by the businessman/bibliophile John Danz, of Baltimore and Chestertown.

8. See, e.g., George P. Landow's *Hypertext* (Baltimore, Johns Hopkins University Press, 1992).

9. Notably by Gilles Deleuze and Felix Guattari, e.g. in *A Thousand Plateaus: Capitalism and Schizophrenia* (Minneapolis: University of Minnesota Press, 1987).

10. Borges was all but blind.

JOHN BARTH, one of the preeminent writers of our time, was born in 1930 in Cambridge, Maryland, on the Eastern Shore of the Chesapeake Bay. A winner of the National Book Award for fiction, he is the author of fourteen novels and short-story collections, as well as two collections of nonfiction. Barth, a Senior Fellow at Washington College, lives in Chestertown, Maryland.

MARY RHINELANDER is an artist and illustrator in Chestertown whose work has included portraits of such literary figures as Nathaniel Hawthorne and Walt Whitman. Rhinelander holds art degrees from Harvard University, Tufts University and the School of the Museum of Fine Arts in Boston, where she studied printmaking.

THE LITERARY HOUSE PRESS, founded in 1994 by faculty, staff and students at Washington College in Chestertown, Maryland, has published more than a dozen works of fiction, poetry, history, essays and travel writing. The Press recently published *Browsing* in hardcover as its first fine letterpress limited edition, of which this offset paperback edition is a facsimile.

COLOPHON

Book design and composition by James Dissette
using Macintosh systems and Pagemaker 7.
The typeface is Dante, designed by
Giovanni Mardersteig at the Officina Bodoni
and redrawn by Monotype's
Ron Carpenter for digital applications.
Printed by Kent Printing, Chestertown, Maryland.

*This edition of Browsing was made possible by a grant from
the Sophie Kerr Committee of Washington College.*